To Dale and E...
my brother an...
in Chris...

The Scarlet Cord

Foreshadows of Christ – a Mystery Revealed

Thank you for your endorsement for this book —

Jerry

JERRY ALLEN

Unless otherwise indicated, Bible quotations are taken
from the New International Version, Copyright 1993
by International Bible Society.

ISBN: 1-4392-5521-0
ISBN-13: 9781439255216

Visit www.booksurge.com to order additional copies.

Comments by others who have read The Scarlet Cord

"The validity of the Christian faith rests on the identity of Jesus Christ. Is he the Messiah of whom the ancient prophets wrote? Is he unique in all of history? Don't form an opinion without taking into account the facts presented in this book."

Dennis Cochrane—*Minister-at-Large, Wycliffe Bible Translators*

"Jesus Christ is a priceless treasure waiting to be discovered by those who eagerly seek for Him. I am confident that all readers of this book will enjoy discovering the great treasure of Christ in page after page, story after story, of God's revelation of Himself and His Son."

Brian G. Fisher—*Senior Pastor, Grace Bible Church, College Station, Texas*

"For years I have watched as Jerry Allen and his wife, Jan, have been faithful servants of the Lord throughout the United States, Papua New Guinea, and beyond. The Lord has used Jerry to teach others how to dig deep into the Scriptures, a fact that is apparent in this book.

"*The Scarlet Cord* is a beautiful example of Jerry's ability to open the Scriptures, explore their profound truths, and explain them with clarity and power. The doctrine is sound, the application is good, and the interpretation is true.

"I look forward to seeing how the Lord uses this book to encourage and challenge individuals in their understanding of the deep truths found within the Scriptures."

Luis Palau—*World Evangelist*

"To all who would love to understand more fully the miraculous unity of the Word of God and its unswerving elevation of Jesus Christ, *The Scarlet Cord* is for you. This book draws our hearts to Jesus and helps us see again the certainty that 'in everything He might have the supremacy' (Colossians 1:18).

"Our entire church family is enriched by Jerry and Jan's faithful example of a lifetime given in service to their Master, and now we rejoice in this work that so clearly reveals and exalts Christ. As you read these timeless truths, may you come to love more deeply the One who gave Himself for you—and the world."

Carl Palmer—*Pastor-Teacher, Cedar Mill Bible Church, Portland, Oregon*

"The many precise prophecies and 'types' for Christ in the Old Testament not only provide unmistakable proof that Jesus is our Savior, but also give beautiful insights into His character and work. This thorough yet concise study of Old Testament pictures of our Lord will stimulate both your appreciation of Christ and of the Scriptures."

Dick Patty—*former international director for Cadence.*

"We never realized how many parallels there were between our Lord and Joseph! *The Scarlet Cord* is a challenge to the non-believer and a source of assurance to the Christian."

Dale and Elaine Rhoton—*founding member of Operation Mobilization, and author, respectively.*

CONTENTS

DEDICATION

This book is dedicated to the faculty of Multnomah University (formerly Multnomah School of the Bible), who were the first to teach me the unity of the Scriptures and among the first to model for me the supremacy of Christ.

It is also dedicated to Papua New Guinean cotranslators and colleagues on Buka and Bougainville islands. My wife, Jan, and I have worked with them for many years, under the auspices of the Wycliffe Bible Translators, helping to translate the Bible into minority languages of that region. Their enthusiasm for the seminars I gave in 2008 on Old Testament previews of Christ has encouraged me to put the material into book form.

ACKNOWLEDGMENTS

Many thanks to all those who have helped in the various stages of preparing the manuscript of this book for publication. Aretta Loving and Jenny Evans have given invaluable input on the editing side. I am very grateful to my wife, who has spent many hours reading the manuscript and suggesting improvements on content, style, and formatting. My gratitude to our grandson, Aaron Shelton, who did the cover illustration. Most of all, I give thanks to my heavenly Father, who gave me the inspiration and the enablement to write this book.

EXPLANATORY NOTES

Some Bible passages are referred to indirectly and are not enclosed in quote marks. Though a Bible reference is normally given in each case, the passage is not a direct, word-for-word quote unless bracketed by quote marks.

Editorial words or phrases, marked by square brackets [ ], are inserted occasionally for clarification.

ABBREVIATIONS

(primarily for use in charts)

Bible Books

Gen	Genesis	Mt	Matthew
Ex	Exodus	Mk	Mark
Lev	Leviticus	Lk	Luke
Num	Numbers	Jn	John
Deut	Deuteronomy	Ac	Acts
Jos	Joshua	Rom	Romans
2 Chr	2 Chronicles	1 Cor	1 Corinthians
Ps	Psalm	2 Cor	2 Corinthians
Isa	Isaiah	Gal	Galatians
Jer	Jeremiah	Eph	Ephesians
Ezek	Ezekiel	Pp	Philippians
Am	Amos	Col	Collossians
Mic	Micah	1Tim	1 Timothy
Zec	Zecharaih	Heb	Hebrews
		1 Pet	1 Peter
		2 Pet	2 Peter
		1 Jn	1 John
		Rev	Revelation

Bible Versions

EB	The Everyday Bible	NLT	New Living Translation
JBP	J.B. Phillips	REB	Revised English Bible
MSG	The Message	TEV	Today's English Version

Other

OT	Old Testament	BC	Before Christ's birth
NT	New Testament	AD	After Christ's birth

PREFACE

Many years ago while serving with the U.S. Navy in the Philippines, I attended a servicemen's conference and heard someone teach about Joseph (son of Jacob) as a man whose life foreshadowed that of Christ. As a young Christian, I had never heard that kind of teaching before. I was amazed at the number of similarities between those two men, despite a gap between them of some 1700 years! I am also amazed that, even today, I never hear a sermon preached on the subject. I had not seen a book about this kind of comparison until I was overseas in 2008 and, in a bookstore, just "happened" to see (and buy) a used copy of an old book, *The Cross and it's Shadow*. The main topic of that book concerns things and people in the Old Testament that prefigure the Messiah. The Old Testament provides many examples of this kind of comparison, and yet people say very little about it today. So I thought it was time for someone to write a book about these amazing previews of our Messiah—experienced and written many centuries before he was born.

The Scarlet Cord illustrates the constantly recurring biblical theme of God's plan of salvation for all who believe, and how the Old Testament symbolizes and previews it in various ways. This book provides clear evidence to skeptics of the credibility of the Scriptures and the truth of God's Word, and explains the implications one by one. It also encourages God's people to further their knowledge of God and his Word and to pursue spiritual maturity, experiencing a deeper walk with Christ.

Even if you don't read the Bible or see any relevance it has for your life, I am asking you to look into the pages of this book and give it a chance to communicate some surprising truths to you. Read the following chapters with an open mind, and let the evidence in the pages of the Bible speak for itself.

I told you these things long ago;
before they happened I announced them to you...
From now on I will tell you of new things,
of hidden things unknown to you.
Isaiah 48:5-6

Everything that was written in the past
was written to teach us,
so that through endurance
and the encouragement of the Scriptures
we might have hope.
Romans 15:4

Jesus Christ...
the mystery hidden for long ages past,
but now revealed.
Romans 16:25-26

PROLOGUE

Eliab and Jesher moved cautiously through the hills, avoiding the more traveled roads, and approached the city of Jericho. Eliab said, "We can't draw attention to ourselves. Let's find a place to stay where no one will suspect we are on a mission for General Joshua."

Jesher whispered, "Keep your ears open. We need to get a feel for this place and what these people think about the Hebrews. Use your best Canaanite. We can't give them any clue we are Jews."

Eliab replied, "We've disguised ourselves as best we can, but you're right, our Hebrew accent mustn't give us away. If we pretend we have colds we won't have to talk too much."

They entered the city for the first time. Strange people, strange ways of dressing, an idol here and there. Some people looked at them curiously. Others ignored them. They cautiously inquired and were told of an innkeeper named Rahab who would probably take them in for the night. Once they located the inn they found there was a vacancy. In the corner there was a small table where they could eat and inconspicuously catch snatches of other people's conversations.

Later, when they were in their room, someone knocked at the door. "Who is it?" Eliab asked.

"A message for you." They opened the door and recognized Rahab's trusted servant. He made sure no one else was nearby, then whispered, "Rahab wants you to meet her on the roof immediately. Your safety depends on it! There's a stairway at the end of the hall."

When the messenger left, Eliab and Jesher looked at each other. "Do you think it's a trap?" Jesher asked.

Eliab was already pondering that, "I got the distinct impression earlier that Rahab sympathizes with us. She seems to have a fear of our God that the other Canaanites don't. For our own good we'd better take a chance and respond to her request. Otherwise we could be in real trouble."

They made sure no one was in the hallway. Then they left, one at a time, and went up to the roof, where they found their hostess waiting for them. They sat down near the stalks of flax she had laid out to dry.

Rahab whispered, "Hide yourselves! No one should see you here. Someone saw you in the street and rumors are afloat. When my servant was at the well she heard women talking about spies. By now I expect the king knows! Quick, get under this flax and lie still. Some of the king's men will probably be here any minute. I'll be back later after they've gone."

Without hesitation they crawled under the flax and lay flat. Debris fell across their faces and they closed their eyes, barely breathing under the scratchy stalks. Rahab pulled more flax over her visitors, satisfying herself that no one could see them. Then she quickly slipped away.

After some time they heard her voice, "It's OK. You can come out now. They're gone."

Eliab and Jesher crawled out, relieved to breathe the fresh air again. She said, "I diverted them to the road that leads to the fords of the Jordan. I know Yahweh has given this land to you Hebrews. The people in Jericho—and those in the surrounding areas— are afraid of you. We've heard how the Lord dried up the water of the Red Sea for you when you came out of Egypt, and what you did to the two kings of the Amorites east of the Jordan! Everyone's afraid of you now, because your God rules heaven and earth. Please promise me that you'll protect my family, because I've protected you. Swear to me that you won't kill my father and mother, my brothers and sisters, or any of my relatives."

"OK. Our lives for your lives," the men swore to her. "If you don't tell what we're doing, we'll save you and your family when the Lord gives us the land."

Then Eliab pulled out a scarlet cord from under his clothing and handed it to her. He said, "We aren't obligated to keep the promise unless you put this cord in your window where we can see it when we return with our people. Hang it in this window where we are going to climb down to escape. All your family have to come here to your house." Then, touching the cord he'd given her, he added, "And remember, this scarlet cord means your salvation. When our people see it, they'll know not to kill anyone in this house."

Rahab responded without hesitation, "I agree. We'll do everything you said."

Since Rahab's house was part of the city wall, Eliab and Jesher rappelled down from her outside window, and escaped into the night. Rahab watched them go, then tied the scarlet cord in that window.

After Joshua heard the two men's encouraging report, he led all the Hebrews across the Jordan River. When the people of Jericho heard that the Hebrews were on the west side of the Jordan and coming toward them, they closed and locked the town gates. No one could enter or leave. They posted extra sentries on the walls and more watchmen on the towers. Surely, they thought, the Hebrews couldn't breach their fifteen foot high and five foot thick walls that surrounded the town.

At God's command, the Hebrews marched around the city of Jericho once each day for six days, with the Ark of the Covenant and seven priests carrying seven trumpets—all bracketed by soldiers. On the seventh day they circled the city seven times. Suddenly the priests blew the trumpets, all the Hebrews shouted, and the walls of Jericho collapsed! But the part of the wall that housed Rahab and her family remained intact! As the Hebrews went in and began destroying the city, Eliab and Jesher saw the scarlet cord and remembered the promise they had made to Rahab. And they rescued Rahab and her family.

One small red cord, symbolizing a respect for and a faith in the God of Abraham, Isaac and Jacob, made all the difference for Rahab and her family.

1

I MAKE KNOWN THE END
FROM THE BEGINNING
Isaiah 46:10

The theme song for a translators' training course in Papua New Guinea in 2008 was "Ancient Words." The words of God, though ancient, are forever fresh. They not only foreshadow the Savior of the first century but also relate to us in the twenty-first century. This chapter briefly discusses the antiquity of the Old Testament Scriptures that point toward a future fulfillment, then introduces the One they point to.

Ancient words

Many Old Testament passages were written hundreds of years before the events they foreshadowed occurred. Actual historical events, corroborated by archeological evidence, demonstrate that many things predicted in earlier centuries actually happened much later.

Of the almost 900 Dead Sea Scrolls, about 220 of them are biblical manuscripts, which constitute our earliest witnesses to the antiquity of scriptural texts. Paleographers have established that some of these documents—copies of earlier manuscripts originally written by biblical authors—were made several hundred years

BC (Flint). This supports the claim that Old Testament prophecies date well in advance of their New Testament fulfillment.

∽

Old Testament prophecies date well in advance of their New Testament fulfillment.

Among the Dead Sea Scrolls archeologists found a complete copy of the Hebrew text of the book of Isaiah, which contains many prophecies about the Messiah. Paleographers date the copy around 125 BC, making it more than 1000 years older than any previously possessed (McDowell, p. 78). This replicates an earlier scroll of the same Isaiah text that traces back to the original manuscript Isaiah himself wrote. Isaiah's ministry began about 740 BC, the year King Uzziah died (Isaiah 6:1), and Isaiah himself died about 680 BC. The New Testament often quotes or alludes to Isaiah, which testifies to the New Testament authors' acceptance of the book of Isaiah as inspired of God and an important part of the Old Testament Scriptures.

Selected scholars translated the Septuagint—the Greek translation of the Hebrew Scriptures—during the reign of King Ptolemy Philadelphia of Egypt between 285 and 246 BC. The Samaritan Pentateuch, an early copy of the Hebrew text of Genesis to Deuteronomy, also dates several hundred years BC (McDowell, pp. 82, 85). This provides further support for the antiquity as well as the integrity of the Old Testament writings.

A number of psalms predict the Messiah (see following chapter). The latest is probably Psalm 137, a song of lament clearly written during the days when the Hebrews were being held captive by the Babylonians in the sixth century BC. Some unknown editor probably compiled the psalms in their present form shortly after the captivity ended about 537 BC (www.gotquestions.org).

Fulfilled in Christ

Now let's look at the One the Old Testament Scriptures point toward. Was Jesus Christ the Messiah? I once encountered a young man who said, "People don't emphasize Jesus enough." He contended that Christians emphasized the Pauline and other epistles too much. So he decided God had inspired only the words of Jesus himself, and he ignored the rest of what we know as Scripture. On the other hand some people say, "He was only a man, just a prophet." I have met likeminded people over the years who say people emphasize Jesus too much. "The Bible," they say, "talks about a lot of other things besides Jesus." I agree with the latter statement, but I don't agree with the idea that we make Jesus too important. In this book there is ample evidence that Jesus Christ is not only central to the Scriptures but also central to God's plan of salvation through the ages.

When a person with expressive talent wants to talk or write about someone he loves, admires or considers important, he often uses many colorful terms and figures of speech to describe that person. The Song of Solomon is an example. In the same way the Scriptures

∽

The grand primary object of all Scripture is to testify of Jesus.

George P. Landow

describe Jesus Christ as the promised Messiah by many names, prophecies and types. (A "type" is something in the Old Testament that foreshadows something in the New Testament.) The Bible emphasizes his greatness and the many facets of his character and glory. The multiplicity of descriptions underscore his importance in history.

George P. Landow, Professor of English and the History of Art, Brown University, said this:

> The grand primary object of all Scripture is to testify of Jesus. Old Testament ceremonies are shadows of Christ. Old Testament judges and deliverers are types of Christ. Old Testament history shows the world's need of Christ. Old Testament prophecies are full of Christ's sufferings, and Christ's glory yet to come.

In Isaiah 41:4 God said, "Who has done such mighty deeds, directing the affairs of the human race as each new generation marches by? It is I, the Lord, the First and the Last. I alone am he" (NLT). And Jesus said in Revelation 1:17, "I am the First and the Last." So it was not a difficult thing at all for God to reveal ahead of time, in different ways, what his Messiah would be like.

The Scarlet Cord describes prophecies, stories and rituals in the Old Testament that foreshadow the Christ of the New Testament. It focuses on things and actions in the Old Testament that prefigured Christ, as well as on people who were types of Christ. The Old Testament authors could see only vaguely the significance of all this, but the One who inspired them understood it clearly. In the Old Testament we see only a dim preview of the far greater glory and meaning of God's ultimate plan of salvation through Christ.

2

THE ONE WHO WAS TO COME
Luke 7:19

God said in Isaiah 48:5, "I told you these things long ago; before they happened I announced them to you." God knows what will happen in the future, so it is not difficult for him to announce ahead of time through his prophets things that will happen at a later time. Prophecies and types share a common component: both point to something in the future. The following text describes prophecies which relate to the Messiah.

The word "Christ" is from the Greek word *Xristos*—a translation of the Hebrew word *Mashiach*, from which we get our English word "Messiah." This title means "God's anointed one" or "the one God appointed."

The Old Testament contains many prophecies about Christ. For example, Isaiah 7:14, 9:6 and Micah 5:2 fore-tell Christ's birth; Isaiah 11:1-5 and 61:1-2, his life and ministry; Isaiah 53 and Zechariah 13:7, his death. At one point Jesus took his twelve apostles aside and said to them, "We are going up to Jerusalem, and everything that is written by the prophets about the Son of Man will be fulfilled" (Luke 18:31). When Jesus used the term "Son of Man," he was referring to himself.

The Messianic Psalms

According to Halley (p. 250), many psalms, some written as early as 1000 years before Christ, contain references to the Messiah that are fulfilled in the person of Jesus Christ. The eleven psalms that are most clearly Messianic are:

Psalm 2	Deity of the Messiah
Psalm 8	Lord of creation
Psalm 16	Resurrection
Psalm 22 and 69	His suffering
Psalm 45	His majesty
Psalm 72	His eternal reign
Psalm 89	God's oath
Psalm 110	King and Priest
Psalm 118	To be rejected
Psalm 132	Inheritor of David's throne

Isaiah 9:6

A close examination of a prophecy about Christ (for example, Isaiah 9:6) can narrow down, detail by detail, who may or may not be the fulfillment of the prophecy:

For to us a child is born, to us a son is given,
and the government will be on his shoulders.
And he will be called Wonderful Counsellor,
Mighty God, Everlasting Father, Prince of Peace.

- *For to us* (initially the Jews). The Messiah would be a Jew.
- *a child is born*. He would begin life as a baby, not appear miraculously as an adult.
- *a son is given*. He would be a male. No female Messiah.
- *the government will be on his shoulders*. He would be a political leader.
- *he will be called Wonderful*. He would be beyond explanation.
- *Counsellor*. He would be a wise man.
- *Mighty God*. He would have a divine nature.
- *Everlasting Father*. He would be identified with the first person of the Trinity and would live forever.
- *Prince of Peace*. He would be associated with peace—first peace with God, then leading to peace of heart and eventually to peace on earth among mankind.

This eliminates the great majority of people as candidates for the position of Messiah. But many more fulfilled prophecies of Jesus' life and death narrow the Messiah down to only one person.

Isaiah 53

One of the most amazing chapters in the Bible is Isaiah 53, which describes in graphic detail the ultimate sacrifice that the Messiah would make for us. This chapter is not about the nation of Israel. It is about an individual. The prophet Isaiah wrote this prediction between about 700 and 680 BC. And yet it spells out clearly what would happen to Jesus Christ some 700 years later. These things were actually fulfilled by Jesus. Following are some of the main passages:

Isaiah 53 fulfilled in Christ

OT Ref.	OT Text (Prophecy)	NT Ref.	NT Text (Fulfillment)
Isa 53:3	He was despised and rejected by men.	Mt 27:39	Those who passed by hurled insults at him.
Isa 53:7	He was oppressed and afflicted, yet he did not open his mouth.	Mt 27:12	When he was accused by the chief priests and the elders, he gave no answer.
Isa 53:5	The punishment that brought us peace was upon him, and by his wounds we are healed.	Mt 27:26	[Pilate] had Jesus flogged, and handed him over to be crucified.
		1 Pet 2:24	He himself bore our sins in his body on the tree...by his wounds you have been healed.
Isa 53:12	He bore the sin of many, and made intercession for the transgressors.	Lk 23:34	Jesus said, "Father, forgive them, for they do not know what they are doing."
Isa 53:12	He poured out his life unto death, and was numbered with the transgressors.	Rom 4:25	He was delivered over to death for our sins.
		Mt 27:38	Two robbers were crucified with him, one on his right and one on his left.
Isa 53:9	He was assigned a grave with the wicked, and with the rich in his death.	Mt 27:57-60	Joseph, a rich man from Arimathea ...took [Jesus'] body...and placed it in his own new tomb (NLT).

The twenty-nine prophecies

Max Lucado makes a compelling comment in his book *The Next Door Savior* (p. 147):

> "More Old Testament foretellings were realized during the crucifixion than on any other day. Twenty-nine different prophecies, the youngest of which was five hundred years old, were completed [fulfilled] on the day of Christ's death."

∽

Christ fulfilled twenty-nine prophecies in one day!

—Josh McDowell

What are the odds against eight prophecies (made by man without inspiration from God) being fulfilled in one lifetime? Lucado (p. 147) summarizes mathematician Peter Stoner:

> "Cover the state of Texas two feet deep in silver dollars. On one dollar place one mark. What is the probability that a person could, on the first attempt, select the marked dollar? Those are the same odds that eight prophecies would be satisfied in the life of one man."

But, according to Josh McDowell (pp. 183-192), Christ fulfilled twenty-nine prophecies in one day! Six of these are shown in the Isaiah 53 chart above. Following are several other examples of prophecies fulfilled during the last 24 hours of Christ's life.

Other fulfilled prophecies of Christ's death

OT Ref.	OT Text (Prophecy)	NT Ref.	NT Text (Fulfillment)
Ps 69:4	Those who hate me without reason outnumber the hairs of my head. Many are my enemies without cause, those who seek to destroy me.	Jn 15:24-25	Jesus said, "They have seen these miracles, and yet they have hated both me and my Father. But this is to fulfill what is written in their Law: 'They hated me without reason.'"
Zec 13:7	Strike the shepherd, and the sheep will be scattered.	Mk 14:27, 50	"You will all fall away," Jesus told them, "for it is written, 'I will strike the shepherd, and the sheep will be scattered.' ... Then everyone deserted him and fled.
Ps 69:21	They put gall in my food and gave me vinegar for my thirst.	Jn 19:28-29	Later, knowing that all was now completed, and so that the Scripture would be fulfilled, Jesus said, "I am thirsty." A jar of wine vinegar was there, so they...lifted it to Jesus' lips.
		Mt 27:34	There they offered Jesus wine to drink, mixed with gall.

Ps 22:7-8	All who see me mock me. They hurl insults, shaking their heads, "He trusts in the Lord, let the Lord rescue him. Let him deliver him, since he delights in him."	Mt 27:41-43	The chief priests, the teachers of the law and the elders mocked him. "He saved others," they said, "but he can't save himself…He trusts in God. Let God rescue him now if he wants him."
Ps 22:1	My God, my God, why have you forsaken me?	Mt 27:46	Jesus cried out in a loud voice… "My God, my God, why have you forsaken me?"
Ps 34:20	He protects all his bones, not one of them will be broken.	Jn 19:33, 36	When they came to Jesus and found that he was already dead, they did not break his legs… These things happened so that the scripture would be fulfilled: "Not one of his bones will be broken."
Zec 12:10	They will look on me, the one they have pierced.	John 19:34, 37	One of the soldiers pierced Jesus' side with a spear…as another scripture says, "They will look on the one they have pierced."

The crucifixion of live criminals was unknown in the Old Testament. The closest anyone came to crucifying people was to hang the bodies of executed (stoned) criminals on trees as a warning. So, considering this, Old Testament passages that allude to crucifixion are that much more amazing.

Clearly these prophecies come from God and not from man. In no way could their fulfillment be the result of mere chance. There should be no doubt that they are divinely inspired. And not included here are many other prophecies relating to Christ's birth, nature, life and ministry. In fact, the Old Testament contains more than 300 references to the Messiah that were realized in Jesus Christ! (McDowell, p. 168)

These fulfilled prophecies leave no room for doubt that God inspired the Old Testament writers. And in subsequent chapters, we will see other things in the Old Testament that give evidence that God was at work preparing people for the coming of his Son.

3

A SHADOW OF THE THINGS THAT
WERE TO COME
Colossians 2:17

This book is about types of Christ in the Old Testament; that is, things or actions or people that prefigure the Messiah. The book focuses particularly on foreshadows of the life and death of Jesus Christ. First, I comment briefly on biblical symbolism, then I endeavor to more clearly define "type."

The Bible is full of symbols. *The Merriam-Webster Dictionary* defines "symbol" as "something concrete that represents or suggests another thing that cannot in itself be pictured." For example, in the Bible, a lion is a symbol of, among other things, regal power; burning incense is a symbol of prayer; a scepter, a symbol of political authority. According to Peter Masters, symbolism was a popular teaching method in the Middle East. That is one reason types and symbols occur so frequently in the Bible. The symbolism of ancient non-Hebrew cultures represents the ideas and philosophy of man. Biblical symbolism is superior in that it represents revealed truth.

Some things are symbolic of Christ, as was the bronze snake in the wilderness. In faith and obedience people looked to that symbol and God saved them from death.

It is a type of Christ, previewing the One who would save from sin all who would trust in him.

Bauer (p. 747) defines the Greek word *semeion* (often translated as "sign") as a "distinguishing mark by which something is known." In the New Testament this Greek word often refers to something unusual or miraculous that associates a particular person, message or action with God. In John 6:30-31 the people asked Jesus for a sign (*semeion*) that he was the Messiah. The NIV Study Bible notes here, "A popular Jewish expectation was that when the Messiah came he would renew the sending of manna." Jesus responded by saying, "The bread of God is he who comes down from heaven." So the manna of the Old Testament was a type of Christ as the One who had come from God (see chapter 4). In Matthew 12:38-40 Jewish leaders again asked Jesus for a sign (*semeion*) , and he referred to the sign of Jonah, who was a foreshadow of Christ (see chapter 6).

According to James Orr (p. 3029), other Greek words also convey the general idea of "type" or "likeness." One is *skia* ("shadow"). It implies dimness, but also suggests some resemblance between two things. Another Greek word is *hupoderigma* ("copy," "pattern"). This denotes a sketch or draft of something future.

The English word "type" derives from the Greek word *tupos*, which New Testament versions variously translate as "figure," "pattern," "manner," "form," "example," "type" and similar renderings. The words share the meaning component of "likeness." Many things in the Old Testament resemble things in the New Testament. The earlier example corresponds to the later reality, so there is a similarity between the two. This is the basic meaning of a type.

🖎

These are a shadow of the things that were to come. The reality, however, is found in Christ.

Louw defines the Greek word *tupos* as "a model or example which anticipates or precedes a later realization." He associates it semantically with words like figure and pattern. Adam, in Romans 5:14, is a figure (*tupos*) of one who was to come (Christ). Different English versions variously translate the Greek word *tupos* in Romans 5:14 as "type," "figure" (or "prefigure"), "pattern" and "foreshadow."

The New Testament contains many examples of Old Testament types that prefigured Christ. Colossians 2:16-17 refers to them as "shadows": "Do not let anyone judge you by what you eat or drink, or with regard to a religious festival, a New Moon celebration or a Sabbath day. These are a shadow of the things that were to come. The reality, however, is found in Christ." Hebrews 10:1 supports this: "The law is only a shadow of the good things that are coming—not the realities themselves."

Hebrews 9:23 uses the word "copies": "It was necessary, then, for the copies of the heavenly things to be purified with these sacrifices, but the heavenly things themselves with better sacrifices than these." In the context of chapter 9, the idea of "better sacrifice" clearly refers to Christ.

When I was a Boy Scout I learned about different kinds of trees, how they are identified and distinguished. I would look at the shadow of a big tree and get some idea of what it was like. But I learned much more about the tree when I went up close, felt its bark, examined its leaves, and observed its fruit. The tree itself became much more meaningful than just its shadow. It is the same with a type. It is a similitude of the thing it points ahead to. But the reality it represents is far greater than its shadow.

⁓

> **Types had the seeds but not the details of the reality they symbolized.**
>
> *—Peter Masters*

God used Old Testament object lessons, based on real people and historical events (not on myths), to prepare people for his plan of salvation. Ritual and sacrifice began to reveal this amazing plan, and later Christ himself consummated it by fulfilling what these things anticipated. Orr (p. 3029) states that the Mosaic system was like a school that trained the Jewish people in the things of God. It also taught them to look for better things to come. It is as if God taught his people their letters in the Old Testament, and in the New Testament he teaches them to put the letters together to spell CHRIST!

According to Dr. Peter Masters, types had the seeds but not the details of the reality they symbolized. They trained the minds of the Old Testament believers to expect such things as substitutionary atonement, though they could not fully comprehend it. Types indicate that the New Testament was where the Old Testament was headed. And they were designed to fully authenticate Christ when he came.

∽

Types indicate that the New Testament was where the Old Testament was headed.

Of course, we could easily identify too many things as types of Christ. We have to be careful to avoid this. In the early centuries of the Christian church, some of the church fathers found "types" in every biblical incident and event, however minor. Most everything was over-spiritualized. Now, in the twentieth and twenty-first centuries, many biblical scholars go to the other extreme. They unduly restrict the kinds of things they think typify Christ. Some say only the Old Testament prefigures of Christ referred to as such in the New Testament are legitimate types of Christ. But in fact, those are only samples of a much larger inventory of types of Christ found in the Old Testament. So we need to have a balance here and we need to use our God-given common sense. Later in this book it will become obvious that, while there is not an inexhaustible supply of types of Christ in the Old Testament, there are certainly some types that are not referred to in the New Testament.

What are the criteria for identifying a "type" as such? Orr (p. 3029) states that true types share three distinctive features. (1) A type is a true, though incomplete, picture of whatever it represents. For example, Aaron as high priest was a type of Christ the Great High Priest. The Day of Atonement is a true picture of the atoning work of Christ. (2) A type always prefigures something in the future. In this sense, a type of Christ and a prophecy of Christ are similar in function but different in form. (3) A true type is divinely inspired and even planned. Because there were centuries of time separating the types from their future realities, only an omniscient God not limited to time could design the earlier to be an unmistakable representation of the later. Only God can make true types!

How are types classified? There seems to be four basic kinds: things, rituals, people, and events. (1) Some examples of *things* (inanimate) that are types of Christ are: Jacob's stairway, the bronze snake, the Rock of Horeb, the pillar of cloud and fire, and the manna. (2) *Ritual* (action) types have to do with such things as the offerings, the scapegoat and the Passover. (3) *People* (personal) types are those whose experiences preview the life or times of Christ and/or truths relating to God's plan of salvation for mankind. Some examples of this are Isaac, Joseph, Moses and David. (4) *Event* (historical) types are real events that foreshadow God's plan of salvation and/or the Christian life; for example, the Exodus and deliverance from bondage in Egypt, the wilderness journey, and the conquest of Canaan. This book focuses on the first three points. Historical types are beyond its scope.

If the New Testament refers to something in the Old Testament, even with only one or two similarities, as symbolizing Christ, then I propose that it qualifies as a true type. There is an explicit and inspired correlation between the two. Jonah is an example.

Jonah and Christ

Jonah	Similarity	Christ
Jonah 1:17; Mt 12:40	Was in death or its shadow for 3 days and 3 nights.	Mt 12:40
Jonah 3:4-5, Mt 12:41	Preached the Word of God.	Mt 4:17

But there are also types that are not mentioned in the New Testament as such. Joseph, the great-grandson of Abraham, is an example (illustrated later in this book). But if something that prefigures Christ in the Old Testament is not in the New Testament as a fore-shadowing, how do we know if it is a true type? I suggest a three similarity rule.

Years ago I learned in the study of anthropology that it could be considered coincidental if two stories from different tribes or in different languages have one or two motifs that are the same. But if the same two stories have three significant motifs that are the same, it likely indicates the stories came from the same original source. (For example, both stories are about a woman by herself conceiving children, about two brothers, and about one person deceiving another.) I suggest we can apply the same principle to types of Christ. When you compare something in the Old Testament (not mentioned in the New Testament) to Christ (e.g. a story), one or two similarities may be coincidental. But if there are three or more significant similarities, then perhaps it is something more than just two stories that have similarities. You also apply, of course, the three criteria for identifying a type mentioned above.

The red heifer of Numbers 19:1-22 is another example of a type of Christ not mentioned in the New Testament. The following chart shows several similarities between the red heifer and Christ, which, according to the above criteria, qualifies the red heifer to be a type of Christ (Haskell pp. 146-152).

The red heifer and Christ

The red heifer (Numbers 19)	Christ
The heifer was to be without blemish (v 2).	Christ had no sin (2 Cor 5:21).
It was to be an animal who had always been free (v2).	The Son of God came of his own free will and died so that we may be free from sin (Heb 10:5-7).
It was killed outside the camp (v 3).	Jesus was crucified outside the city, signifying that he died not only for the Jews but for the whole world (Heb 13:12).
The ashes of the heifer represented cleansing from defilement (v 9).	The blood of Jesus purifies us from all sin (1 Jn 1:7).

4

COPIES OF THE HEAVENLY THINGS
Hebrews 9:23

Biblical types represented truths that in the Old Testament times people could not fully understand. Consequently the thing that some types pointed to is called a "mystery." In this chapter we will look at some inanimate things that are types of Christ.

Jacob's stairway

In John 1:51 Jesus said to Nathanael, "You shall see heaven open, and the angels of God ascending and descending on the Son of Man."

In Genesis 28:10-17, Jacob, when on his way to Paddan Aram, had a dream. In the dream he saw a stairway connecting heaven and earth, and angels were going up and coming down on it. God was at the top of the stairway and repeated to Jacob the same promise he had given his grandfather Abraham and his father Isaac. When Jacob woke up he said, "How awesome is this place! This is none other than the house of God, this is the gate of heaven!" And he named that place Bethel, which means "house of God."

The following chart shows how the stairway in this dream was a type of Christ.

Jacob's stairway and Christ

Jacob's Stairway (Genesis 28)	Christ
The stairway connected earth and heaven (v 12).	Christ is the way to God (Jn 14:6). As the only Mediator between God and man (1 Tim 2:5), he reconciles man with God.
God was visible at the top (v 13).	Because of Christ's sacrifice, heaven is open and God is accessible (Mt 27:50-51).
Angels were ascending and descending (v 12).	Christ provides constant access to God and communication with God (Jn 1:51).

The bronze snake

When the people of Israel complained in the wilderness against Moses and God (Numbers 21:4-9), God sent poisonous snakes among them. Many were bitten and died. The people appealed to Moses, and God told him to make the figure of a snake as a remedy. So Moses made a bronze snake and put it on a pole. Anyone who had been bitten by a snake and who looked at the bronze snake was healed, and he lived. In John 3:14-15 Jesus said, "Just as Moses lifted up the snake in the desert, so the Son of Man must be lifted up, that everyone who believes in him may have eternal life." So Jesus acknowledged this Old Testament symbol as a representation of himself.

The manna

Jesus had an informative and revealing conversation with the crowd in John chapter 6. Some Jews said to Jesus (verse 31), "Our forefathers ate the manna in the desert; as it is written, 'He gave them bread from heaven to eat.' " (Psalm 78:24-25 refers to manna as "the grain of heaven...the bread of angels.") Jesus said to them, "It is my Father who gives you the true bread from heaven. For the bread of God is he who comes down from heaven and gives life to the world" (verses 32-33). Then he said, "I am the bread of life...I am the bread that came down from heaven" (verses 35, 41). So the manna, which maintained physical life, was a figure of the Messiah, who would come down from heaven and be the source of spiritual life.

The cornerstone and the stumbling stone

> ∽
>
> Our forefathers drank from the spiritual rock that accompanied them, and that rock was Christ.

"I am placing a stone in Jerusalem that causes people to stumble, and a rock that makes them fall. But anyone who believes in him will not be disappointed" (Romans 9:33, NLT). The author to the Romans here quotes from Isaiah 8:14 and 28:16. An NIV Study Bible note on Romans 9:33 states, "The two passages from Isaiah, which are here combined, apparently were commonly used by early Christians in defense of Jesus' Messiahship." The idea of "stumbling" is a metaphor for taking offense at Christ and his message. But the phrase "anyone who believes in him will not be disappointed" shows that there is a positive side also to this "stone."

Jesus said, "The stone the builders rejected has become the capstone" (Matthew 21:42). This capstone (or cornerstone) could refer to one of three stones: a large, horizontal lintel over a door; the middle stone of an arch; or a large stone used to anchor and align the corner of a wall. In any case, Jesus was referring to himself as the capstone. In 1 Peter 2:4-8, for those who believe, Christ becomes the cornerstone, precious and foundational to their faith. But for those who do not believe, the same stone becomes a stumbling stone. Luke 20:17-18 reiterates this same dichotomy.

The rock at Horeb

In 1 Corinthians 10:1-4 the apostle Paul states, "Our forefathers...drank from the spiritual rock that accompanied them, and that rock was Christ." Here the author explicitly refers to a rock as a type of Christ. Paul was referring to the rock at Horeb in Exodus 17:6. God provided the rock from which came the water that the Israelites needed to live. And Jesus is the living water of John 4:10-14.

The Tabernacle

Dr. Lewis Sperry Chafer, in his book *Systematic Theology* (p. 125), made an informative comment (summarized here) about the Tabernacle as described in Exodus 25:1 to 40:38:

> The Tabernacle provides an extensive typology of the Old Testament. The Tabernacle itself is a type of Christ as the only way to God. The Ark of the covenant sprinkled with blood is the place where peace is made with God. The bread of the Presence is a type of Christ as the Bread of Life given for the world. All references to silver allude to redemption. The bronze altar represents judgments against sin which Christ bore in his death. The candlestick is a type of Christ as the Light of the world. The golden altar represents that aspect of Christ's death which was a sweet incense

to God. And the bronze basin foreshadows cleansing through the blood of Christ.

The Ark of the Covenant

God commanded Moses to make a chest (ark) of acacia wood and overlay it with gold (Exodus 25:16). He was to put into the chest the Ten Commandments to represent his covenant with the people of Israel. And the Messiah would later institute the new covenant (Isaiah 42:6). Then Moses was to make a gold atonement cover (mercy seat) for the chest, including two cherubim overshadowing the chest with their wings. (Cherubim were celestial beings symbolized as protectors of God's holy things.) The atonement cover represented the presence of God (Exodus 25:17-22). This is where temporary atonement would be made for sin (Hebrews 10:11). Christ became the permanent atonement for our sin (Romans 3:25; Hebrews 10:12, 14).

Granted that these things are types of Christ, how do we know that certain similarities between the Old Testament and the New Testament are not just coincidental? Perhaps this story will help.

> One winter night in Minnesota, a woman was driving on a country road in a snowstorm. It was a whiteout, snow mixed with fog. She couldn't see more than a few feet ahead, and wasn't quite sure where she was. She cranked up the car heater and the loud blowers were

reassuring. She prayed to God for guidance. Suddenly a rabbit hopped out in front of the car. She was able to stop in time to miss it since she had been going slow anyway. She inched the car forward but the rabbit didn't move aside. He just hopped back and forth in the middle of the road immediately ahead of her. She honked her horn, but the rabbit just sat there twitching its whiskers at her. It was not going to let her pass. She was getting impatient and thought, *Move you silly rabbit. I'm tired and cold and need to get home.*

Suddenly the ground shook. There was a loud noise and a flashing light. A freight train roared by right in front of her! She had been just about to cross a railroad track without knowing it! No warning light and no gate indicated a railroad crossing. She probably would have been hit and killed if the rabbit hadn't stopped her. When the train had gone by, the rabbit hopped out of the road and disappeared into the bush, its mission accomplished. (This true story is summarized from the February 2009 issue of *Guideposts* magazine.)

Was what happened in this story just a coincidence? Some would say "Yes." Others would not be sure. And some would say, "No, the hand of God was protecting that woman." In the same way, some will look at these things in the Old Testament and say, "They just happened by chance." Others will say, "Maybe there is more than just

∽

> God must have had a hand in setting up such an amazing pairing of types and their fulfillment.

coincidence in this story." And for those who are still skeptical, I will be giving ample information on types in the following chapters. For some of the more significant types in the Old Testament, the evidence is overwhelming that these passages clearly prefigure the coming Messiah, fulfilled by Jesus Christ himself. They indicate that God must have had a hand in setting up such an amazing pairing of types and their fulfillment.

5

WITHOUT THE SHEDDING OF BLOOD THERE IS NO FORGIVENESS
Hebrews 9:22

Certain rituals were very important to the Jews, and had meaning far beyond what a casual observer would perceive. Examples are circumcision, different kinds of cleansing, special religious days and feasts. This chapter focuses on specific Jewish rituals that prefigured the Messiah.

On the one hand, sacrifices and offerings as types are only an approximation of the thing or person they point toward. The fulfillment of a type has far greater significance than that which symbolizes it. True believers in the Old Testament knew that types were not the essence of the spiritual truths they symbolized. David wrote in Psalm 51:16-17, "You do not delight in sacrifice or I would bring it; you do not take pleasure in burnt offerings. The sacrifices of God are a broken spirit; a broken and contrite heart, O God, you will not despise" (cf. Matthew 9:13). The offerings themselves were not the ultimate answer. They alone could not atone for sin. If they could, the author of the book of Hebrews would not have written, "It is impossible for the blood of bulls and goats to take away sins" (Hebrews 10:4).

On the other hand, Old Testament types offer much detail that is not available in the New Testament. Their descriptions continue to enrich the meaning of what they anticipated. So a study of types can give us further glimpses into the significance of what they symbolize. An example is how the offerings in the Old Testament show different aspects of the salvation we have in Christ.

Offerings

The book of Leviticus gives details regarding the offerings acceptable to God. The main theme of Leviticus is holiness—the holiness of God and the necessity for man to be holy in order to approach God. Physical perfection symbolizes spiritual holiness (NIV Study Bible introduction to Leviticus). Not only the priests had to be ceremonially clean, but also their clothes, the instruments they used, and the sacrifices they offered. And we know that Jesus Christ was without sin, the perfect sacrifice on behalf of mankind.

Why did God establish such an intricate sacrificial system? According to Masters, it was to show the character of human sin and the difficulty of atoning for it. He describes five kinds of offerings, listed in Leviticus 1-7. There are more than five, but these five, listed below, all have an element of atonement in them, and each in some way complements the others. The offerings were all animal sacrifices except the grain offering, which consisted of fine flour. Very poor people were allowed to substitute an offering of fine flour in place of an animal (Leviticus 5:11).

The *burnt offering* was the only offering where a whole animal was offered. It represents the consecration of the entire person, wholly dedicated to God. Christ also was wholly consecrated to God, an offering of perfection on our behalf. "You were redeemed...with the precious blood of Christ, a lamb without blemish or defect" (1 Peter 1:18-19); "You are not your own. You were bought at a price" (1 Corinthians 6:19-20). God transfers my failure and sin to Christ, the perfect offering and acceptable substitute for me. The blood of the offering represents a life given for a life. The continually burning fire represents God's unchanging holiness. And the sweet savor represents acceptableness.

The *grain offering* was partly burned and partly eaten. It signifies refinement. We should have a refined Christian character, developing the attitude of Christ (Philippians 2:5). We should possess virtues that exemplify the fruits of the Spirit (Galatians 5:22-23). Our character should be a testimony of what God is like.

Part of the *peace or fellowship offering* was for God, but most of it was eaten. It represents fellowship, reconciliation, and unity. Christ himself is our peace, and it is he who unifies his people (Ephesians 2:14).

The *sin offering* was for all actual sins—sins of ignorance and willful sins. It was also for ceremonial uncleanness. We can incur sin by associating with evil. Christ bore the sins of many (Isaiah 53:12). "God made Christ, who never sinned, to be the offering for our sin, so that we could be made right with God through Christ" (2 Corinthians 5:21, NLT); "He himself bore our sins in his body on the tree, so that we might die to sins and live for righteousness" (1 Peter 2:24).

The *guilt or trespass offering* made restitution for violating God's holy things (even unknowingly) or for sins against other people. Jesus the Messiah is our guilt offering. Isaiah 53:10-11 reads, "Though the LORD makes his life a guilt offering…the will of the LORD will prosper in his hand…by his knowledge my righteous servant will justify many, and he will bear their iniquities." To "justify" means to declare "not guilty."

Abel's offering

Chafer (p. 119) describes Abel's offering as a type of Christ. I have summarized his description here:

> Abel's offering (Genesis 4:4) merits the favor of Jehovah. It indicates that God had given instruction on the importance and value of blood sacrifices to the first of the race as they emerged from the Garden of Eden. By this sacrifice, Abel obtained witness that he was righteous. In this connection, we will do well to read Hebrews 11:4 and 9:22b, as well as all Scripture relating to the importance of sacrificial blood. This doctrine is not of human origin, and its fulfillment in the death of Christ is alone the plan and purpose of God.

The scapegoat

Leviticus 16:5-26 describes the scapegoat ritual as part of the Day of Atonement. There were actually two goats in this ceremony. One became a sin offering to the Lord. They preserved the other goat alive before the Lord and used it for making atonement by sending it into the desert as a scapegoat. Chafer (pp. 122-123) makes the following comment on the topic of the Day of Atonement:

> "The larger extent and accomplishment of Christ's death is set forth typically in magnificent detail by the events and specific requirements of the Day of Atonement...The specific features thus required are: the bullock for the high priest, the substitution of the animal for the sinful person, the upholding of the law, the perfect character of the sacrifice, the sin covered by the blood of the first goat, and the guilt taken away by the dismissal of the second goat."

The goat they kill represents Christ's death (Scofield, pp. 147-148), which vindicates the holiness and righteousness of God (Romans 3:24-26). The living goat represents that aspect of Christ's work which takes away our sins from before God (Hebrews 9:26; Romans 8:33-34).

The Passover

Chafer also makes the following comment (pp. 120-121):

"Israel's national and abiding redemption, as well as the safety of the firstborn in each home, was secured by the paschal lamb. So far-reaching is this redemption that Israel was required, in recognition of it, to re-enact the Passover throughout all her generations— not as a renewal of redemption, but as a memorial. The two general aspects of the meaning of the Passover are also well expressed by C.H. Mackintosh" (summarized below):

The paschal lamb is the ground of peace and the center of unity. The blood on the door posts secured Israel's peace. The death sentence had been handed down. But God in his mercy found an unblemished substitute for Israel. So God's claims and Israel's need were met by the same thing, the blood of the lamb. But the Israelites also gathered in fellowship around the roasted lamb. And apart from the perfect atonement of Christ, there could be no fellowship either with God or His people. But Jesus said, "Where two or three come together in my name, there am I with them" (Matthew 18:20).

The Passover and Christ
A comparison of two sacrifices

The Passover (Exodus 12)	Christ
A lamb to be offered (v 3, 6)	Jesus, God's Passover lamb, takes away the sin of the world (Jn 1:29; 1 Cor 5:7).
The lamb was killed on the Passover, the first month of the year (v 2), the beginning of the Jewish calendar.	Jesus was crucified on the Passover (Jn 19:13-14), and his birth marks the beginning of the Christian calendar.
A year-old male without defect (v 5)	Jesus was in the prime of life, without sin (Heb 4:15).
A substitute for the people (v 23; Lev 17:11)	Christ is our substitutionary atonement (1 Jn 2:2).
They were to eat the meat of the lamb (v 8).	Jesus said, "Take and eat, this is my body" (Mt 26:26).
Do not break any of the bones (v 46)	They didn't break Jesus' bones (Jn 19:33, 36; cf. Ps 34:20).
They were to put the blood on the sides and top of the door frame—the shape of a cross (v 7).	Jesus shed his blood on the cross (Col 1:19, 20).
God said, "When I see the blood I will pass over you. No destructive plague will touch you when I strike Egypt" (v 13).	The blood of Jesus cleanses those who believe from all sin, and they are not condemned. (1 Jn 1:7; Jn 5:24).

In Matthew 26:26, Jesus was inaugurating the Lord's Supper (the Christian Communion), in which the bread and the wine represents his body and blood, sacrificed for the people of the world.

Now one can hardly doubt that Jesus Christ is the fulfillment of all that the Passover typified.

∾

> The theme of redemption is like a scarlet cord tying together many prophecies, symbols, rituals and stories in the Bible.

What do these types and parallels teach about God, his Word, and his relation to man? For one thing, they show that the Bible has a central and timeless theme, repeated throughout the Scripture: **redemption** through the sacrifice God has provided. That theme of redemption is like a scarlet cord tying together many prophecies, symbols, rituals and stories in the Bible. They describe and predict God's amazing plan of salvation for mankind, and show his wisdom in making a way for people to be reconciled to him. They depict the many ways in which God was preparing people for His Son, whom he would send to die for the sins of the world and be raised again victorious over sin and death.

6

A BETTER HOPE IS INTRODUCED
Hebrews 7:19

Many individuals in the Old Testament are types of Christ. Abraham, as one who believed God, was similar to Christ in various ways, and his most famous descendant was the Messiah. Boaz was the kinsman redeemer in the book of Ruth. David was like Christ in many ways, and later also his son, Solomon. (For other names, see chapter 11.) Space does not allow showing in detail how all these men prefigured Jesus the Messiah. But the following text briefly discusses Jonah, Noah, Aaron and Melchizedek as types of Christ. Later the book will discuss in more detail three men (Moses, Joseph and Isaac) and show many parallels between them and Christ.

Jonah as a type of Christ

In Matthew 12:38-41 the Jewish religious leaders asked Jesus to give them a sign that he was the Messiah. Jesus replied that he would give them only the sign of the prophet Jonah: "As Jonah was three days and three nights in the belly of a huge fish, so the Son of Man will be three days and three nights in the heart of the earth." Jesus was referring to his own death and burial.

Then he said that the men of Nineveh, who repented when they heard Jonah's message, would condemn the people of his (Jesus') generation. This clearly implied that the people of Jesus' generation had not repented, even though they were hearing and witnessing Someone greater than Jonah.

So we can confidently conclude that what Jonah did and what happened to him constitutes a type of Christ. (See chart in chapter 3.)

It is clear, however, that Jonah did not at all times typify Christ. He was fallible, as we all are. Chapter 1 of the book of Jonah describes how he disobeyed God. Chapter 4 shows how he complained and pouted when God didn't destroy Nineveh. This behavior certainly did not foreshadow Christ. But part of his life and experience was a type of Christ, and that is the part Jesus referred to in Matthew 12.

Noah as a type of Christ

The Bible honors Noah as a righteous man. Ezekiel 14 lists him along with Job and Daniel as a model of righteousness. Hebrews 11:7 describes him as a man of faith: "By faith Noah, when warned about things not yet seen, in holy fear built an ark to save his family. By his faith he condemned the world and became heir of the righteousness that comes by faith." Also in Matthew 24:37-39, Jesus said the godless mindset of the people in his own time was similar to that of the people in Noah's time—they were unaware of and unprepared for the coming judgment. So Noah was another who prefigured Christ.

Noah and Christ

Noah	Similarity	Christ
Heb 11:7	He had faith in God and obeyed God.	Jn 8:28-29
Ezek 14:14, 19	He was declared righteous by God.	Mt 3:17
2 Pet 2:5	He was a preacher of righteousness.	Mt 4:17
Heb 11:7	He prepared the means of saving people.	Heb 10:5-7
Heb 11:7	By his righteous life he condemned the unbelieving world.	1 Jn 2:1; Jn 3:18

Aaron and Melchizedek as types of Christ

According to Exodus 19:6, the nation of Israel was to be a kingdom of priests. But the Messiah would be the High Priest who would atone for the sins of the world, as prophesied in Isaiah 53:4-12 (NIV Study Bible note on Isaiah 42:1-4). Both Melchizedek, during the time of Abraham, and Aaron, during the time of Moses, were priests. In this respect they were similar to Christ. Aaron represented the Levitical priesthood, but Melchizedek represented a priesthood of a higher order. They also compared with Christ in other ways.

Aaron

In the very act of going into the Holy of Holies once a year, Aaron, in what he did and who he was (the high priest), shows three ways that he was a type of Christ. (The room in the Tabernacle, and later in the Temple, that represented the presence of God was called the Holy of Holies.) The sacrifice Aaron carried in with him was a type of Christ. The Ark of the Covenant was a type of Christ. And since Aaron was a high priest, he himself was a type of Christ. But Christ's priesthood is superior in every way to the Aaronic priesthood, as is illustrated in the following chart.

Melchizedek

Melchizedek is at the same time one of the most obscure and one of the most important persons in the Bible. He appeared only once, and then briefly. He met Abram (later renamed Abraham) returning victoriously from a battle (Genesis 14:18-20): "Then Melchizedek, king of Salem, brought out bread and wine. He was priest of God Most High, and he blessed Abram, saying, 'Blessed be Abram by God Most High, Creator of heaven and earth. And blessed be God Most High, who delivered your enemies into your hand.' Then Abram gave him a tenth of everything." (Salem was an early name for Jerusalem.)

> ∽
>
> God allowed imperfect people to be types of his perfect Son.

Aaron and Christ

Ref.	Aaron	Christ	Ref.
Heb 7:20-21	Aaron became priest without an oath.	Christ became priest with an oath made by God himself.	Heb 7:20-21
Heb 5:1-4	Aaron, brother of Moses, was the first high priest.	Jesus, the Son of God, is the last High Priest.	Heb 5:5-6; 6:20
Heb 7:23	Aaron represented a temporary, changing priesthood.	Christ has a permanent, unchangeable priesthood—he is a priest forever.	Heb 7:17, 24
Ex 28:1; Num 3:5-10	Aaron's priesthood was limited to the nation of Israel.	Christ's priesthood is for the whole world, for all who will trust him as their Messiah.	Jn 17:20
Deut 18:1-5	Aaron was a Levitical priest, but not a king. Royalty did not belong to the tribe of Levi.	Christ, from the tribe of Judah, is both priest and king. Royalty belongs to the tribe of Judah.	Heb 7:14-17; Rev 19:16
Num 16:46-48	Aaron prayed for his people during his lifetime.	Jesus Christ is praying for his people now and forever.	Jn 17:8-11; Heb 7:25
Heb 7:27	Aaron offered sacrifices many times for the sins of the people and for himself.	Jesus offered himself as the sacrifice once for all time and for all people who would accept him.	Heb 7:27

Heb 9:7	Aaron went through the veil once a year, which separated the Holy Place from the Holy of Holies. It represented a barrier between the holiness of God and the sinfulness of man.	At Jesus' death, the veil, the curtain of separation, split in two from top to bottom. This signifies that God has permanently opened the way into his presence and has dealt effectively with sin.	Mk 15:38; Heb 10:19-22
Heb 9:7-8	On the people's behalf, Aaron approached the Ark of the Covenant, which represented the presence of God.	Jesus ushers believers into the very presence of God.	Heb 6:19-20; 9:24
Lev 16:15-16	Aaron sprinkled the blood of the sacrifice on the mercy seat for the remission of Israel's sins.	Jesus shed his own blood to redeem from sin all those who trust in him.	Heb 9:27-28

It was not until about 1000 years later that the Scripture mentions Melchizedek again. Psalm 110:4 says, "The LORD has sworn and will not change his mind: 'You are a priest forever, in the order of Melchizedek.' " In the context of Psalm 110, God was saying this to the One who would become the Messiah. After that, the Scripture is silent again in regard to Melchizedek for about another 1000 years, until the book of Hebrews was written. That occurred sometime between the death of Christ (about 30 AD) and the destruction of Jerusalem in 70 AD.

Most types of Christ relate directly to Christ and have no intermediary type in between. But Melchizedek was an intermediary type between Aaron and Christ in that, in some ways, he more closely represented the priesthood of Christ than Aaron did. Hebrews 7:17-19 speaks to this. The text first says of the Messiah: "You are a priest forever, in the order of Melchizedek." Then it says, "A better hope is introduced, by which we draw near to God" (cf. Hebrews 4:16 and 6:19-20). Melchizedek was a sign to the Old Testament Hebrews that something better was coming—something greater than Aaron and the Levitical priesthood. And this Something greater would be associated with the coming Messiah. In the New Testament this is part of the "Mystery" that Jesus Christ revealed and fulfilled.

None of these people who constitute types of Christ were perfect or worthy of being compared with the Messiah. Even Melchizedek, about whom we know very little, was human and therefore fallible. They all made mistakes, and sinned in one way or another. God not

Melchizedek and Christ

Ref.	Melchizedek	Christ	Ref.
Heb 7:1	Was both priest and king	Is both priest and king	Heb 7:17; Rev 19:16
Heb 7:1-2	King of righteousness and king of peace	Prince of peace and king of righteousness	Isa 9:6-7; Jer 23:5-6
Heb 7:3	Figuratively "without father or mother, without genealogy, without beginning of days or end of life"	Literally a priest forever	Heb 5:5-6

only allowed imperfect people to be types of his perfect Son, but in many cases he planned it that way. No one can say God engineered the imperfections, but he does use them to emphasize how much greater and more wonderful his Son is when compared to his human counterparts.

We can only conclude that when we count the many different types of Christ in the Old Testament and their significance, the evidence of Christ's supremacy becomes overwhelming!

༄

> ༄
>
> Only he who knows the end from the beginning could have planned such parallels as these over a period of many centuries.

These prophecies and types in the Bible not only present a continuing theme of redemption, but also demonstrate that **God is eternal**. Only he who knows the end from the beginning could have planned such parallels as these over a period of many centuries. God has many titles, but only one name: Yahweh (Jehovah). It means "I am" when he is speaking of himself, and "He is" when another is speaking of him. He always lives in the present and encompasses the past and the future in the "now." Jesus said, "I am the Alpha and the Omega [the A and the Z]...the First and the Last...the Beginning and the End" (Revelation 1:8, 17; 22:13). "Jesus Christ is the same yesterday and today and forever" (Hebrews 13:8). He and God the Father belong both to the Old Testament and to the New.

7

GOD WILL RAISE UP FOR YOU A PROPHET LIKE ME
Deuteronomy 18:15

Moses himself foreshadowed the One who would come after him. In Deuteronomy 18:18 the Lord said to Moses, "I will raise up for [the Israelites] a prophet like you from among their brothers. I will put my words in his mouth, and he will tell them everything I command him." This other prophet was to be none other than Jesus Christ the Messiah. He would be the ultimate prophet, and would in some ways resemble Moses. The Jews were looking for that prophet (John 1:21) but did not recognize him when he came. The book of Hebrews describes Jesus as one not only like Moses but also superior to him in every way.

Moses' life began in a similar way to Jesus' life. A political leader tried to kill him as an infant, but God protected him. Moses grew up in Egypt, and later, by God's power and direction, led the people of Israel out

> ⌒
>
> The Lord said to Moses, "I will raise up for [the Israelites] a prophet like you from among their brothers."

of Egypt and out of bondage. God gave Israel his Law through his servant Moses, who also served as a prophet, a priest, a judge, an intercessor and a mediator. God even used Moses at times to control the elements.

The following chart illustrates various ways in which Moses was a type of Christ. The multiplicity of significant similarities leave no doubt that Moses was truly a prefigure of the One who was to come after him.

By now it should be clear that these similarities are not coincidental. The parallels between Moses and Jesus didn't happen by chance. Moses wrote the Pentateuch (Genesis to Deuteronomy) some 1400 or 1500 years before Jesus was born. There is no way Moses could have known the details of Jesus' life. It is obvious that God planned it this way.

ᘒ

The writing and composition of so many books over such a large span of time that agree in all the essentials can only be inspired by the God who planned for it to eventually be one book—his book.

The books of the Bible were written in Hebrew or Greek, with some passages in Aramaic, by many different authors over hundreds of years. In spite of this diversity, the foregoing parallels indicate that **the Bible is essentially one book**. It ultimately has one Author, the God of heaven and earth, the God of the ages. The writing and composition of so many books over such a large span of time that agree in all the essentials can only be inspired by the God who planned for it to eventually be one book—his book.

Moses and Christ
A comparison of two ministries

Ref.	Moses	Christ	Ref.
Ex 1:22-2:10; Ac 7:20	Pharaoh tried to kill Moses, an extraordinary child, but failed.	Herod tried to kill Jesus, an extraordinary child, but failed.	Mt 2:13-15; Lk 1:31-33
Heb 11:26	Moses regarded disgrace for the sake of Christ as having greater value than the treasures of Egypt.	Christ "set aside the privileges of deity and took on the status of a slave."	Pp 2:6-7 (MSG)
Jos 1:1-2	The Lord referred to Moses as, "Moses my servant."	God said of Jesus: "Here is my servant whom I have chosen."	Isa 42:1; Mt 12:18
Ex 18:13	Moses served as judge for the people.	God has given Jesus authority to judge because he is the Son of Man.	Jn 5:27
Ac 7:36	Delivered people from physical bondage.	Delivers believers from spiritual bondage.	Lk 4:18; Rom 6:17-18
Ex 34:28	Fasted 40 days and nights on Mt. Sinai.	Fasted 40 days and nights in the desert of Judea.	Mt 4:2
2 Cor 3:7-8	Moses' face was radiant.	Jesus' face shone like the sun.	Mt 17:2

Deut 18:15	Moses said to the Israelites, "The Lord your God will raise up for you a prophet like me from among your own brothers."	Surely this [Jesus] is the Prophet who is to come into the world.	Jn 6:14; 4:25-26
Ps 99:6	Moses and Aaron were among his priests.	Because Jesus lives forever, he has a permanent priesthood.	Heb 7:24
Ex 17:4	Moses cried out to the Lord, "What am I to do with these people? They are almost ready to stone me."	At this, they picked up stones to stone him, but Jesus hid himself, slipping away from the temple grounds.	Jn 8:59
Ex 14:21	Moses stretched out his hand over the sea, and all that night the Lord drove the sea back with a strong east wind and turned it into dry land.	What kind of man is this [Jesus]? Even the winds and the waves obey him!	Mt 8:27
Ex 20:19	They said to Moses, "Speak to us yourself and we will listen. But do not have God speak to us or we will die."	There is one God and one mediator between God and men, the man Christ Jesus.	1 Tim 2:5
Gen-Deut	Author of the Pentateuch, who brought the Law	The Divine Word, who brought grace and truth	Jn 1:1,14,17

8

ONLY WITH RESPECT TO THE THRONE WILL I BE GREATER THAN YOU

Genesis 41:40

Genesis (chapters 37, 39-50) relates the story of Joseph, who lived sometime between 1700 and 1600 BC. He was a favorite son of his father, the eleventh of twelve sons of Jacob (called Israel). In many ways Joseph's life paralleled that of Jesus Christ.

As a teenager Joseph dreamed that all his brothers' sheaves of grain bowed down to his. He also dreamed that the sun, the moon and eleven stars bowed to him.

∽

In many ways Joseph's life paralleled that of Jesus Christ.

These dreams implied he would eventually rule over his brothers and even his parents. His father became curious and his brothers became angry and jealous. So his brothers secretly sold him as a slave when he was seventeen years old. His buyers took him to Egypt and there God blessed Joseph, even as a slave. But he was falsely accused, and, though innocent, was put in prison.

Then God blessed Joseph in prison, and enabled him to correctly interpret the dreams of two other prisoners: the cupbearer and the chief baker—former head servants of Pharaoh, king of Egypt. The cupbearer dreamed he saw three grapevine branches and saw himself squeezing grape juice into Pharaoh's cup. The chief baker dreamed he had three baskets of bread on his head and birds ate the bread from the top basket. Joseph interpreted the dreams to mean that three days later the cupbearer would be restored to his original position and the chief baker would be executed. And these things happened three days later just as Joseph had predicted.

Some time after that, officials released Joseph from prison in order to interpret two dreams of Pharaoh. He had dreamed about seven skinny cows eating seven fat cows. In another dream he saw seven thin heads of grain eating seven healthy heads of grain. And he didn't know the meaning of either dream. Joseph correctly interpreted both dreams as predicting seven years of plentiful harvest followed by seven years of drought. And he proposed a detailed plan to set aside food in the plentiful years to provide for food in the drought years. So Pharaoh promoted Joseph to the second highest position in Egypt.

Then, just as Joseph had predicted, there came seven years of plenty. He ordered much grain to be stored for future use. Then seven years of famine came, also as Joseph had predicted. But because of Joseph's divinely inspired foresight, enough food was available for everyone. So God used Joseph to save the lives of thousands of people.

Events in Joseph's life reveal two major truths. He became a key figure in the survival of his people, the descendants of his father, Israel. And he himself became a type of Christ. Many events in Joseph's life would foreshadow events in the life of Jesus Christ. The following chart shows significant parallels between Joseph and Jesus, some of them striking.

Joseph and Christ
A comparison of two lives

OT Ref. (Genesis)	Joseph	Christ	NT Ref.
37:3	Joseph was especially loved by his father Jacob.	Jesus was especially loved by his Father God.	Mt 3:17
37:8,11	His brothers were jealous of him and hated him.	The Jewish leaders were jealous of Jesus and hated him.	Jn 15:24-25
37:8,18	His brothers did not want him to rule over them, and planned to kill him.	The Jewish leaders did not want Jesus to be the king of the Jews, so they planned to kill him.	Mt 27:1; Jn 19:15
37:28	They sold Joseph as a slave for 20 pieces of silver.	Jewish leaders paid Judas 30 pieces of silver to betray Jesus.	Mt 26:14-15
37:36 (cf. Ex 13:19)	He was taken to Egypt in his youth, but was eventually buried back in Canaan (Israel)	Jesus was taken to Egypt as a child, but later returned to Israel.	Mt 2:13-15, 19-21
40:2-3, 21-22	Two criminals were imprisoned with Joseph, one was forgiven, the other not.	Two criminals were crucified with Jesus, one was forgiven, the other not.	Lk 23:32, 39-43

Reference	Joseph	Jesus	Reference
Chapters 37, 40-41	He interpreted dreams and could foretell the future.	Jesus was a prophet who could foretell the future.	Mt 24-25
41:46	Joseph was 30 years old when he entered the service of Pharaoh.	Jesus was about 30 years old when he began his ministry.	Lk 3:23
41: 40-41	He was exalted to the highest place in the kingdom next to Pharaoh.	Jesus was exalted to the highest place over all creation next to his heavenly Father.	Pp 2:9; Col 1:15
43:28	Joseph became ruler over his brothers and they all bowed to him.	Jesus Christ is King of Kings, and every knee will bow to him.	Pp 2:10-11
45: 5,7	It was to save lives that God sent Joseph ahead of his brothers.	The Son of Man came to seek and save the lost.	Lk 19:10; Jn 3:17
47:23	Joseph said to the people, "This day I have bought you."	They said to the Lamb [Jesus], "You bought men for God from every tribe."	Rev 5:9 (EB)

∽

The truths and principles of the Scripture are applicable across the centuries of time.

The odds against these similarities between Joseph and Jesus happening by chance are literally billions to one. These things reveal not only the theme of redemption running throughout Scripture, the eternal nature of God, and the amazing unity in the inspired Word of God, but also that **God's Word is relevant** to people of all generations. If God can reach across more than a thousand years of time to show such amazing parallels between the lives of Old Testament characters and the life and death of his Son, then the truths and principles of the Scripture are also applicable across the centuries of time. Human situations change but God remains the same. And basic human nature does not change; it always stands in need of God.

9

GOD HIMSELF WILL PROVIDE THE LAMB
Genesis 22:8

In Genesis 22 we read that God commanded Abraham to take his son Isaac to the region of Moriah and sacrifice him as a burnt offering. Abraham obeyed and took Isaac along with two servants on a three day journey. When they were near the place God had indicated, the servants waited at a certain place. Abraham carried the fire and the knife and Isaac carried the wood. As the two of them walked on, Isaac said, "Father, the fire and wood are here, but where is the lamb for the burnt offering?"

Abraham replied, "God himself will provide the lamb for the burnt offering."

> Now I know that you fear God, because you have not withheld from me your son.

When they arrived at the designated place, Abraham built an altar and prepared to offer his son on it. But an angel of the Lord stopped him. "Now I know that you fear God, because you have not withheld from me your son," the angel said.

Then Abraham saw a ram caught by its horns in a thicket. So he sacrificed the ram instead of his son. And the angel repeated the promise and the blessing God had given Abraham earlier.

Several parts of this Genesis story show parallels between Isaac and Christ. What happened to Isaac in Genesis 22 became a preview of what would later happen to Christ. Just as Abraham offered his son, so later God would offer his Son—the Lord Jesus Christ—who becomes the Savior and Lord of all who trust him. So Isaac typified Christ in two senses: as a person and as an offering. Isaac is a type of the Son who was a willing sacrifice and obedient unto death.

The place in Moriah where Abraham offered Isaac became a sacred place. Many years later King David bought property on Mt. Moriah and dedicated it to the Lord (NIV Study Bible note on 2 Samuel 24:16). Then David's son, Solomon, built the temple there, which was in the city of Jerusalem (2 Chronicles 3:1). And eventually, God's Son—Jesus Christ—was crucified there.

All these things make it evident that God planned events far ahead of time that fit into his purposes. Since he sees the whole picture, **his words are shown to be true**. The many fulfilled prophecies and types show that the Bible is credible and trustworthy.

Isaac and Christ
A comparison of two offerings

Ref.	Isaac	Christ	Ref.
Gal 4:29	Isaac was born by the power of God's Spirit.	Jesus was born by the power of God's Spirit.	Lk 1:31, 34- 35
Rom 9:7-9; Gal 4:23	Isaac was the son of promise.	Jesus was the Son of many promises (prophecies).	Isa Ch 53; Isa 61:1-2; Mic 5:2
Heb 11:18	It was through Isaac that Abraham's descendants (God's chosen people) would be identified.	It is through (faith in) Jesus that people are identified as God's true chosen people.	Jn 1:12; Heb 2:9-10
Gen 22:6	Isaac carried the wood that he would be laid upon as a sacrifice.	Jesus carried the wood (the cross) that he would be sacrificed upon.	Jn 19:17
Gen 22:2,9	Abraham offered his son, Isaac, whom he loved.	God offered his only Son, Jesus, whom he loved.	Jn 3:16; Mt 3:17
Gen 22:2	Isaac was offered on a mountain in Moriah.	Jesus was crucified on a mountain in Moriah.	2 Chr 3:1

Gen 22:11-12	The angel of God stopped Abraham from offering Isaac.	Though an angel strengthened Jesus just before his arrest and crucifixion, nothing could stop God from offering his Son as a sacrifice for us.	Lk 22:42-43; Mt 26:53-54
Gen 22:13	God provided a sheep in place of Isaac.	God provided Jesus himself as the Lamb of God in our place.	1 Pet 1:18, 19
Gen 22 3-5	For three days Abraham considered his son, Isaac as dead.	For three days and nights Jesus was in the grave.	Mt 12:40
Heb: 11:19	Isaac was figuratively resurrected from the dead.	Jesus was literally resurrected from the dead.	Lk 24:33-34; 1 Cor 15:3-4

10

DEEP TRUTHS
1 Timothy 3:9

Now let's review important truths learned from the preceding foreshadows of Christ by restating and expanding some observations already made, with one additional observation.

Parallels between the Old Testament and the New Testament reveal a **central and timeless theme of redemption**, repeated throughout the Scripture. Christ the Messiah is the central topic that unites many writings into a beautiful message of salvation for all who believe. The biblical authors could not have written these stories, rituals and prophecies in the Bible that preview God's amazing plan of redemption without inspiration from a Source higher and wiser than themselves. God wanted to make a way for people to be reconciled to himself. These prophecies and types illustrate the many ways in which God was preparing people to believe in his Son, whom he would send to die for the sins of the world and be raised again victorious over sin and death.

These similarities also show **God's eternal nature**. Only he who knows the end from the beginning could have planned such a pairing of similarities over many centuries. To Moses, God revealed himself as Yahweh (Jehovah), which, when God is speaking, means "I am." God is the eternal one, not limited to time. With him

∞

As we obey what we know from the Scriptures, God reveals more of the meaning to us.

"A day is like a thousand years, and a thousand years are like a day" (2 Peter 3:8). So it is no difficult task for him to predict what is to us the future. It was an easy thing for him to reveal the pattern and plan for Old Testament worship that would be a type of the real thing in heaven. And it is nothing to him to arrange the circumstances in a person's life (for example, Joseph's) to form, centuries in advance, a pattern of things that would happen in his own Son's life as the Messiah. So the fact that these parallels between Old Testament history and New Testament truth are so detailed and accurate is clear evidence that only God could have inspired and planned them so far in advance of the time they would be fulfilled in his Son.

Parallels between the Old Testament and New Testament point to the **unity of the Scriptures**. The Bible is not just 66 books written by dozens of authors in three languages over some 1500 or 2000 years. It is essentially one book. There is no way that such a variety of writings by so many authors over such a long period of time could have so much agreement unless there was a Supervising Editor who put it all together. The Bible is primarily a revelation. As such it requires not only reading and study, but also prayer and getting to know the Author. As we obey what we know from the Scriptures, God reveals more of the meaning to us. And gradually we perceive more and more clearly how it is, in fact, one book—his book.

These comparisons also demonstrate that **God's Word is relevant** to people of all generations. If God has such insight across time, he is also able to look into our individual lives and know what is relevant to us today. Customs and issues and personalities change over the centuries, but human nature does not change. God made us. He holds in safe keeping the original DNA of every individual. He knows our genetic code, what makes us tick, and what we need. And he knows how to remold us into the kind of people who please him. Knowing him and obeying his Word is the ultimate source of joy and fulfillment.

Parallels between the Testaments also show that **God's words are true** and can be trusted. Since he understands the past, lives in the present and controls the future, he knows fact from fiction. He knows what will happen hundreds and thousands of years in advance, so the predictions through his prophets are true. It is his nature to tell the truth. Jesus said, "I am the way, the truth and the life" (John 14:6). God is the Source of truth, his Son embodies the truth, and his Spirit inspires

> The words of an eternal God, whose plan of redemption unifies and makes relevant the truth of the whole Bible, have an authority unmatched by any man.

the truth. Consequently God's message has impeccable credibility. And we have ample evidence to believe that his Son is the One he said he is.

◇

In addition, these similarities and truths confirm the **authority of Scripture**. The words of an eternal God, whose plan of redemption unifies and makes relevant the truth of the whole Bible, have an authority unmatched by any man or human government. God is the One to whom we are ultimately accountable. In Matthew 28:18 Jesus said, "All authority in heaven and on earth has been given to me." God's Son and his Word provide a standard that does not waver with every new opinion or circumstance; it does not move back and forth like a tumbleweed with the ever changing winds. Christ is our Anchor, our Rock. He embodies the truth and is the only one who can point us to ultimate reality. In the end we are responsible to him alone.

Do you have an authority or model that helps you make important decisions, especially the moral ones? Is it the Bible? Is it science? Is it a classical philosopher or a university professor you admire? Is it authors of certain books you have read or actors in certain movies you have seen? Is it a TV personality or a sports star or a friend? Or are your decisions based simply on your own personal experience? Only the Scripture has ultimate answers to puzzling life questions. It provides an authoritative standard by which I can measure myself. It provides a goal toward which I can move. It provides a motivation

∞

The Scripture provides not relative or tentative or theoretical truth, but absolute truth that points toward absolute reality.

for me to emulate someone imminently worthy—Christ himself. It provides a purpose for my life, and enables me to make sense of a lot of the things that are happening all around me. It provides a final word, a conclusion, a closure. It doesn't leave me hanging. It provides not relative or tentative or theoretical truth, but absolute truth that points toward absolute reality.

11

SO THAT IN EVERYTHING HE MIGHT HAVE THE SUPREMACY
Colossians 1:18

The many types and prophecies of Christ fulfilled in the New Testament point to salvation through the Messiah for everyone who believes.

Christ is the common component in all we have been talking about. If God's plan of salvation had a color, I think it would be red, prefigured by the blood of the Old Testament animal sacrifices and realized in the shed blood of Jesus Christ. The many types of Christ, combined with the many prophecies of Christ, strung throughout the Old Testament and fulfilled in the New Testament, point to salvation through the Messiah for everyone who believes. They are like a scarlet cord, binding the Old Testament and the New Testament into one book.

Parallels that typify or anticipate Jesus Christ tie together most if not all the books of the Bible. A few examples:

Genesis (Isaac, Joseph)
Exodus (Moses, the Passover)
Leviticus (the sacrifices)
Numbers (the red heifer, the bronze serpent)
Deuteronomy (a future prophet like Moses)
Joshua (himself a type of Christ)
Judges (Samson)
Ruth (Boaz)
1-2 Samuel and 1-2 Chronicles (David, Solomon)
Job (anticipation of a mediator between God and man)
Psalms (many prophecies about the Messiah)
Isaiah and Daniel (more prophecies about the Messiah)
Jonah (himself)
Zechariah (Zerubbabel).

Halley (p. 20) states, "[Christ's] appearance on the earth is the Central Event of all history. The Old Testament sets the stage for it. The New Testament describes it...Christ [is] the Center and Heart of the Bible, the Center and Heart of History." And he should be the Center and Heart of each one of us.

God inspired all these things in the Old Testament that are fulfilled in Christ and planned them for our instruction and encouragement. They underscore

∾

Jesus Christ is the final, perfect and only sacrifice for sin.

the credibility and the relevance of the Scriptures and of God himself. A correct understanding of the teaching of Scripture verifies that what God says is true. He knows human nature, human needs and human desires. He knows us inside and out. He knows our future, and he knows what it takes to make us right with him. The Scriptures teach all this and much more. They teach the truth, and those who want to know the truth can be sure that these teachings of the Scriptures are timeless and trustworthy.

Some say we are putting too much emphasis on Jesus and making him too important. Are we? Not if the biblical emphasis is to be taken seriously. Looking at the book of Hebrews, Jesus Christ, God's Son, the Messiah, is:

greater than the angels (chapter 1)

greater than Moses (chapter 3)

greater than the Levitical priesthood (chapters 4, 5, 7)

greater than the old covenant (chapter 8)

greater than the earthly sanctuary—the tabernacle or the temple (chapter 9)

greater than the Old Testament sacrifices (chapter 10)

Jesus Christ is greater than all sacrifices combined, because he is the final, perfect and only sacrifice for sin under the New Covenant.

He is the Lamb of God, who takes away the sin of the world.

He is our Creator, our Redeemer.

He is the One who wants us to spend eternity with him.

He is the Author and Finisher of our faith.

He is the head of the church, his body, and in him dwells all the fullness of the Deity in bodily form.

He is the Alpha and Omega, the Beginning and the End.

He is the door, the way, the truth, the life.

He is the bread of life, the living water.

He is the lover of my soul.

He is our Friend, our Savior, our King.

He is the only Mediator between God and man.

He is the King of kings and the Lord of lords.

How can I not give the highest honor to such a One?

How can I not worship him with all my heart?

12

LET US ADVANCE TOWARDS MATURITY
Hebrews 6:1 (REB)

Jesus Christ is the sole fulfillment of the prophecies about the Messiah and the only realization of the types of the Messiah. There is no "type" of Mary, or of Peter or Paul. As far as God's plan of redemption is concerned, there are only types of Christ. He is also the focus of history, the central figure and truth of God's plan to save those who believe. Those who look to another person as messiah or mediator (between God and man) allow that other person to usurp the position that rightfully belongs only to Jesus Christ.

Various miraculous events during Christ's sojourn on earth show that God approved of his Son:

∾

The Mount of Transfiguration signaled a profound change in focus—a watershed moment in history.

At Jesus' birth several events clearly indicated that he was a special child. Angels, as messengers of God, predicted Jesus' conception, announced his birth and facilitated his preservation as a small child. God gave him the name Jesus, which means Savior. When Simeon saw the baby Jesus, he said to God, "My eyes have seen your salvation" (Luke 2:30). And Luke 2:52 says, "Jesus grew in wisdom and stature, and in favor with God and men."

At Jesus' baptism God said to him, "You are my Son, whom I love; with you I am well pleased" (Mark 1:11). The three synoptic gospels (Matthew, Mark and Luke) each witness this important declaration. And John the Baptist deferred to Jesus when he referred to him as the Lamb of God and the Son of God (John 1:29, 34).

At the Mount of Transfiguration, recorded in Matthew 17:1-8, two men appeared with Jesus. Peter, James and John recognized them as Moses and Elijah. Moses represented the Old Covenant. Elijah symbolized the proclamation of God's message through the prophets. In fact, he was the precursor of John the Baptist, who was in turn the forerunner of Jesus Christ. As we have seen, Moses himself was a type of Christ. After Moses and Elijah had disappeared and only Jesus was left with the three apostles, God said, "This is my Son, whom I love; with him I am well pleased. Listen to him!" This signaled a profound change in focus, from the patriarchs and prophets to Christ, from the Old Covenant to the New Covenant—a watershed moment in history.

Events during Jesus' crucifixion underscore how profoundly important to God was the death of his Son. Darkness covered the land for three hours (see Luke 23:44). "The curtain of the temple was torn in two from top to bottom. The earth shook and the rocks split. The tombs broke open and the bodies of many holy people who had died were raised to life" (Matthew 27:51-52).

The curtain in the temple had separated man from the Holy of Holies, the room which represented the presence of God. When the curtain was torn in two, it signified that the way to God was now open, through the death of Christ.

∽

> Jesus—not Abraham, nor Moses, nor Elijah, nor the Law—was now to be the focus of the New Testament believers.

Jesus' resurrection attested to the fact that his was an acceptable sacrifice and that God had won over sin and death by the very act of causing his Son to live again. Jesus further gave witness to this approval and acceptance by ascending back to God his Father (Philippians 2:9-11).

Jesus—not Abraham, nor Moses, nor Elijah, nor the Law—was now to be the focus of the New Testament believers. Hebrews 1:1-2 makes this clear by saying, "In the past God spoke to our forefathers through the prophets at many times and in various ways, but in these last days he has spoken to us by his Son, whom he appointed heir of all things, and through whom he made the universe." Christ has fulfilled the Jewish law; he has accomplished the whole purpose of the law (Romans 10:4, NLT). Hebrews chapters 1-10 show how God's Son is superior to Moses and to the whole system that the Jews had as their context for worshipping God. These things were shadows of the reality that was to come in Jesus Christ. God used these models, as it were, for the time period for which they were intended. But now he has revealed his Son, in all his glory, and God expects us to worship him in spirit and in truth (John 4:23-24). He calls us to embrace the reality of all that the types and the prophecies pointed toward.

In the New Testament we see a transition from the old to the new, from the Old Covenant to the New Covenant, from the physical to the spiritual, from the earthly to the heavenly. And we see an amazing pattern of Jesus fulfilling both the types and the prophecies of the Old Testament. It doesn't mean the old system was wrong. It means the old system is made complete in the One whom it anticipated.

∽

Why live in the shadow of Christ when you can experience the person of Christ?

There are still people who live in the Old Testament and overemphasize the importance of Old Testament rituals, rules and laws. They are seemingly satisfied with the virtual reality when they could have the reality itself. Why choose the preview when you can see the whole movie? Why be content with the model when you can possess the real airplane, or the blueprint when you can have the whole house? Why live in the shadow of Christ when you can experience the person of Christ?

However, we should not discard the Old Testament, but have the same perspective and appreciation of it that Jesus did (see Matthew 5:17-20). It has great value in showing us how God dealt with individuals and with nations. It reveals much about God's character and man's character. God inspired the Hebrews to write and preserve for us the Old Testament Scriptures. They, as well as the New Testament Scriptures, are the inspired words of God (see Romans 3:2). It is through the Hebrew people and the Old Testament Scriptures that we are introduced to the concept of God adopting people as his own, of his giving us a glimpse of his glory, of the foundational Old Testament covenants. The Old Testament imparts to us the Ten Commandments and other laws that give us guidelines for life, holiness, and worship, as well as the many promises that God has given his people (Romans 9:4-5). The Old Testament gives us the patriarchs and the human ancestry of Christ. It is the foundation for the New Testament and provides the background for understanding New Testament truths. The Old Covenant provides the underpinnings for the New Covenant.

We have much to learn from the Old Testament. It contains types and stories and history that give us a fuller understanding of the Messiah. This information is not available in detail in the New Testament. We acknowledge that the Old Testament has a vital place in God's overall plan of salvation and his relationship with man.

Without the Old Testament we—the New Testament believers—are incomplete. We learn so much more about God and his plan of salvation over the ages when we understand more of the significance of the Old Testament rituals, sacrifices, services, feasts, and the furnishings of the tabernacle and the temple. But on the other hand, without the New Testament church and the Messiah fulfilling so many of the Old Testament prophecies and types, they (the Old Testament believers) are incomplete: "God had planned something better for us so that only together with us would they be made perfect" (Hebrews 11:40). For this reason, we need a balance. We need to be multi-directional when we compare the significance of the people, the events and the truths in the Old Testament and in the New Testament. The Bible, God's revelation to man, would be incomplete if we had only one or the other. However, we also need to know God's priorities for our present age.

So I suggest the following:

- When Jesus' teaching is **deeper** than the Old Testament teaching (more substantial or meaningful), follow Jesus rather than merely following the Old Testament. In doing that you will also follow the spirit of the Old Testament teachings rather than the letter.
- When Jesus' teaching is **higher** that the Old Testament teaching (more transcendent), follow Jesus.
- When Jesus' teaching is **broader** than the Old Testament teaching (more inclusive), follow Jesus.
- When Jesus' teaching is **longer** than the Old Testament teaching (eternal as well as temporal), follow Jesus.
- When Jesus himself and what he has done **fulfills** the Old Testament teaching, follow Jesus.

"Oh, what a wonderful God we have!
How great are his riches and wisdom and knowledge!
How impossible it is for us to understand his decisions
and his methods!
For who can know what the Lord is thinking?
Who knows enough to be his counselor?
And who could ever give him so much that he would have
to pay it back?
For everything comes from him.
Everything exists by his power and is intended for his
glory.
To him be glory evermore. Amen."
Romans 11:33-36 (NLT)

13

PUT INTO PRACTICE WHAT YOU LEARNED
Philippians 4:9 (TEV)

*W*ith eyes wide open to the mercies of God, I beg you, my brothers, as an act of intelligent worship, to give him your bodies, as a living sacrifice, consecrated to him and acceptable by him. Don't let the world around you squeeze you into its own mould, but let God re-mould your minds from within, so that you may prove in practice that the plan of God for you is good, meets all his demands and moves towards the goal of true maturity. (Romans 12:1-2, JBP)

You may ask, "How does the message of the preceding chapters apply to me? How are these truths relevant to people at the beginning of the third millennium after Christ?" And my answer would be, "They should encourage you to pursue a higher level of maturity in your obedience to the Savior." We must not be content to be spoon-fed with spiritual baby food, as the author writes about in Hebrews 5:11-6:3.

God's Law and the history of God working in and through his people in the Old Testament is true and instructive. But that is only the preview of a salvation and a spiritual life that is much greater than people in the Old Testament were able to comprehend. That is why the New Testament refers to God's plan of salvation in Christ as "the mystery." God couldn't reveal this mystery in its fullness until Christ came. He didn't "hide" it, he withheld it until the time when at least some people would be ready and prepared to understand and accept it.

As we seriously study the Scriptures, it becomes increasingly clear that there is only one way of salvation in the pages of the Bible, repeatedly illustrated by types and prophecies. Hebrews 2:3 has always been sobering to me: "How shall we escape if we ignore such a great salvation?" The author is referring to the salvation we have available to us in Jesus Christ. It is infinitely greater than any prefigure of it heralded in earlier times. Since it is possible to ignore it, we individually must make a choice. We must decide which way we are going to go—man's way or God's way.

> ⁓
>
> ## Such a great salvation is infinitely greater than any prefigure of it heralded in earlier times.

See to it that you do not refuse him who speaks.
If they did not escape when they refused him who warned them on earth,
how much less will we, if we turn away from him who warns us from heaven?
Hebrews 12:25

God has given us eternal life, and this life is in his Son.
He who has the Son has life;
he who does not have the Son of God does not have life.
1 John 5:11-12

God is pleading with us to choose his way, which is the only way to make peace with him and to be cleansed from our sin (Isaiah 1:18). God not only has given us the ability to hunger and thirst for meaning and purpose in life, but he has also provided the One who embodies the water of life and the bread of life (John 4:13-14, 6:35). Jesus Christ died so that we may have eternal life (John 3:16).

If we confess our sins, he is faithful and just and will forgive us our sins
and purify us from all unrighteousness.
1 John 1:9

If you confess with your mouth, "Jesus is Lord,"
and believe in your heart that God raised him from the dead,
you will be saved.
For it is with your heart that you believe and are justified,
and it is with your mouth that you confess and are saved.
Romans 10:9-10

To all who received him, to those who believed in his name,
he gave the right to become children of God.
John 1:12

Perhaps you have drifted away from God and don't know which way to turn. If so, see Proverbs 3:5-6.

Maybe you are burdened down with worries and don't know how to find relief. Matthew 11:28-30 tells you how.

Perhaps you want to return to God but don't think he will accept you back. Read Luke 15:3-7 and 2 Peter 3:9 and you'll know that he will. Return to Christ and serve him as your Lord and Savior. Only he can restore to you the meaning and purpose for which God has created you.

Words from a hymn by Helen H. Lemmel are fitting here:

> *Turn your eyes upon Jesus,*
> *Look full in his wonderful face.*
> *And the things of earth will grow strangely dim,*
> *In the light of his glory and grace.*

Has Jesus ceased to be the focus of your life? Have you relegated him to second or third place? He took your place on the cross. And now you have the opportunity to take his place and represent him in the new life he has offered you, demonstrating the principle of an exchanged life.

∽

The phrase "Jesus is Lord" should mean he is the CEO of my life, directing my attitudes and decisions.

Perhaps you feel there must be more to the Christian life than you have experienced. What we have learned about Old Testament previews and their realization in Christ shows we can go much deeper in learning about God, Christ, and the Holy Spirit. We can become more mature and effective in our Christian lives (see Ephesians 4:11-16). We need to delve more deeply into the character of God and the relevance of the Word of God for our present generation. We need to study, to pray, to take time to know God and his Word. We, our children and our grandchildren, as believers in Christ, will face more and more opposition. We must put on the armor of God—explained in Ephesians chapter 6—in order to fight the spiritual battle every generation of Christians must face.

No one except God knows what the future will bring or how the attitudes we are developing now will affect our future. He knows our hearts infinitely better than we know ourselves. Only he knows what is going to truly satisfy us. That is why it is so wise to let the Son of God truly be Lord over our lives. As Lord he opens up for each of his privileged children an exciting place in his kingdom. He gives us a part in helping others and bringing them to a place where they know him as Savior and Lord!

What does the phrase "Jesus is Lord" mean? It should mean he is the CEO of my life, directing my attitudes and decisions. As someone said recently, he constructs, not just colors, my worldview. If I say, "Jesus is Lord," it should mean he has veto power in my life. If I want to do something and he doesn't want me to do it, his vote is the only one that counts. If he wants me to do something and I don't want to do it, then I submit my will to his will. Jesus is our role model. He said to God his Father in Luke 22:42, "Not my will, but yours be done."

Genuine disciples of Christ are like mirrors, reflecting the character of Christ, who in turn mirrors God, his Father. The types, before the time of Christ, were like shadows. Now the disciples of Christ, looking back on his life, death and resurrection, are like mirrors (2 Corinthians 3:18). As we are transformed into his likeness, we reflect him, so people in our generation can see what he is like. The Old Testament types foreshadowed who Jesus would be. We now need to reflect who he is.

> The Old Testament types foreshadowed who Jesus would be. We now need to reflect who he is.

If you are a Christian, the truths in this book give you something positive to share with your non-Christian friends. In an age when bad news is rampant and commonplace, it is refreshing to have some good news to share with people. The world is desperately in need of good news. And the conclusions of this book represent the greatest news of all!

EPILOGUE

In the genealogy of Jesus Christ in Matthew 1:5, Rahab, who hid the two Hebrew spies, is listed as an ancestor of Jesus. She was the mother of Boaz and an ancestor of King David, all ancestors of Jesus. Hebrews 11:31 commends Rahab as a model of faith who should be emulated. James 2:25 refers to her as righteous, because by saving the spies, she proved her faith in Yahweh. So Rahab, one saved by the scarlet cord, became an ancestor in the family line of Jesus the Messiah, who saves all everywhere who trust in him.

The scarlet cord, which Rahab hung out of her window so the Hebrews would spare her and her family when God destroyed Jericho, meant salvation for them. Those identified with it were saved from death. This scarlet cord did for Rahab and her family what the blood of the Passover lamb did for the Hebrews just before they left Egypt—as a symbol of faith it saved them from death. And those who put their trust in Christ are saved from sin and eternal death by his sacrifice.

The prophecies and types of Christ in the Old Testament are also like a scarlet cord. They are a preview of the salvation that would later come through Christ, the Son of God. They tie together the stories and teachings of the Old Testament, beautifully picturing God's plan of salvation for the ages. From their earthly viewpoint the people in the Old Testament saw the shadows, and the pattern was far from clear. But from God's perspective, revealed in the New Testament, there is a beautiful design that illustrates how God loves to save all those who trust in Christ. Christ is truly the One who unites and completes the books, the stories, the poetry, the prophecies and the types of the Old Testament by fulfilling all that God predicted about him.

He is before all things, and in him all things
hold together...
For in Christ all the fullness of the Deity lives in bodily
form,
and you have been given fullness in Christ,
who is the head over every power and authority.
Colossians 1:17; 2:9-10

BIBLIOGRAPHY

Bauer, Walter. *A Greek-English lexicon of the New Testament and other early Christian literature.* Chicago: University of Chicago Press, 1979.

Chafer, Dr. Lewis Sperry. *Systematic Theology*, Vol. 3, Ch. 5. Dallas: Dallas Seminary Press, 1948.

Flint, Dr. Peter. Seminar on the Dead Sea Scrolls. Waco, Texas, 2000.

Halley, Henry H. *Halley's Bible Handbook.* Grand Rapids: Zondervan, 1962. (56th printing: 1986)

Haskell, Stephen N. *The Cross and its Shadow.* South Lancaster, Mass.: The Bible Training School, 1914.

Landow, George P. *The Aesthetic and Critical Theories of John Ruskin.* Ch. 5, sec. 2, "Ruskin's 'language of types' and Evangelical readings of scripture." N.pag. [Internet]

Louw, J. P. and E. A. Nida (eds.). *A Greek-English Lexicon of the New Testament based on Semantic Domains.* New York: United Bible Societies, 1988. [*Translators Workplace* CD, n.pag.]

Lucado, Max. *The Next Door Savior.* Nashville: Thomas Nelson, 2003.

Masters, Dr. Peter. A three part seminar: *Types and Shadows of Christ in the Old Testament.* Metropolitan Tabernacle, London, England.

McDowell, Josh. *The New Evidence that Demands a Verdict.* Nashville: Thomas Nelson, 1999.

New International Version Study Bible. Grand Rapids: Zondervan, 1985. (Translators Workplace: International Bible Society, 1993).

Orr, James (ed.). *The International Standard Bible Encyclopaedia,* vol. 5. Eerdmans, 1939.

Scofield, Dr. C. I. *The Scofield Reference Bible.* Oxford University Press, New York: 1917 (London: 1967).